CAMBODIA
The Land and Its People

Text & Photos by **Barry Broman**

Marshall Cavendish
Editions

Front cover: Dancers from the Khmer Dance Ensemble

Editor: Melvin Neo
Designer: Bernard Go Kwang Meng

Published by Marshall Cavendish Editions
An imprint of Marshall Cavendish International
1 New Industrial Road, Singapore 536196

Other Marshall Cavendish Offices
Marshall Cavendish Ltd. 5th Floor 32–38 Saffron Hill, London EC1N 8FH • Marshall Cavendish Corporation. 99 White Plains Road, Tarrytown NY 10591-9001, USA • Marshall Cavendish International (Thailand) Co Ltd. 253 Asoke, 12th Flr, Sukhumvit 21 Road, Klongtoey Nua, Wattana, Bangkok 10110, Thailand • Marshall Cavendish (Malaysia) Sdn Bhd, Times Subang, Lot 46, Subang Hi-Tech Industrial Park, Batu Tiga, 40000 Shah Alam, Selangor Darul Ehsan, Malaysia.

Marshall Cavendish is a trademark of Times Publishing Limited

National Library Board Singapore Cataloguing in Publication Data
Broman, Barry Michael, 1943-
Cambodia : the land and its people / Barry Broman. – Singapore : Marshall Cavendish Editions, 2009.
p. cm.
ISBN-13 : 978 981 4276 53 5 (pbk.)
1. Cambodia – Description and travel. 2. Cambodia – History.
3. Cambodia – Civilization. 4. Cambodia – Social life and customs. I. Title.

DS554.3
959.6 — dc22   OCN436592982

Printed in Singapore by Fabulous Printers Pte Ltd

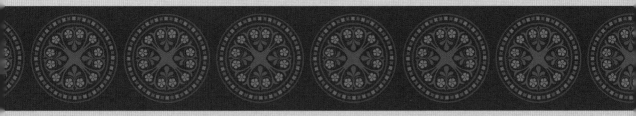

Author's Preface

This photo book gives a visitor or prospective visitor a visual introduction to Cambodia. It is also a useful souvenir of a visit to Cambodia or a gift. It covers the main tourists sights of the kingdom notably the ancient temples in and around Angkor Wat and cultural icons such as the Royal Palace and National Museum in Phnom Penh where photography is normally not allowed.

The book shows Cambodians at work and at play, from farmers and fishermen in fields and rivers to hundreds of thousands gathered at Phnom Penh to celebrate the annual Water Festival, the country's largest.

Some rarely visited sites are portrayed such as the temple of Preah Vihear perched on a cliff top on the Thai border and virtually inaccessible from Cambodia on the plains below. The temple was given to Cambodia in a World Court decision in 1962 but is still a source of friction between the two countries. The remote temple of Banteay Chhmar in the jungle of northwestern Cambodia is depicted, the largest temple of Cambodia never restored. The sapphires mines at Pailin, located in a malarial area near Thailand is included but not recommended as a place to visit.

The text outlines the rich cultural past of Cambodia and its tortured recent history. I lived through much of that history as a journalist and diplomat and have included that perspective in the narrative. I have added some unpublished black and white photographs that I took in and around Cambodia between 1963 and 1991.

Dedication

This book is dedicated to the memory of
Warren Hoffecker who loved Cambodia.

THAILAND
LAOS
Preah Vihear
Banteay Chhmar
Poipet
Sisophon
Angkor Wat
Siem Reap
Tonle Sap
Krong Pailin
Sambor
Kratie
Mimot
Kampong Cham
Tonle Sap
Oudong
PHNOM PENH
N
PichNil Pass
VIETNAM
Kampong Som (Sihanoukville)
Kampot
Kep
Gulf of Thailand

Acknowledgements

The author wishes to thank the following people for their assistance in making this book starting with Wandoeun Kimson "Kim" McDevitt who has been his source of information on things cultural and historical in Cambodia for thirty-five years. Thanks also to Prince Tesso Sisowath, Princess Bopha Devi, HE Kong Sam Ol, Chresten Bjerrum, Paul Strachan, Elizabeth Becker, Roland Eng, John and Sophiline Cheam Shapiro, Stephane Arrii, Bob Peterson and John Stevenson.

Cambodia : *The Land and its People*

On a January day in 1860, a young French naturalist traveling in eastern Siam heard rumors of ancient ruins in the area from a French missionary. Together they crossed the Tonle Sap, the great lake of Cambodia, and ventured up a small stream surrounded by jungle. They happened upon a broad moat near a massive stone temple. The naturalist was Henri Mouhot and the temple was Angkor Wat, the largest religious structure ever constructed.

Massive roots at Ta Phrom temple

Face at the Bayon

The discovery caused a sensation in Europe and began the quest for more information about the civilization that created the temple overrun by an embracing jungle. Mouhot, however, was not among them. Within a year of his find he succumbed to malaria near the royal capital of Laos, Luang Prabang, where his well-tended grave may be seen today on the spot where he died.

Of course the ruins of the great capital of the Khmer Empire were never really lost. Mouhot found Buddhist monks in residence at Angkor Wat. Following the fall of Angkor to invading Siamese forces in the 15th century and its abandonment by Cambodian kings, who relocated their capital further east, the temple had been maintained as a pilgrimage site. Monks are still at Angkor where, surrounded by tourists, they worship images of the Buddha in temples originally built to honor Hindu deities.

During the early centuries of the Christian era, while Rome was in decline, small Hinduized states were emerging in the lower Mekong river valley. The states of Funan and Chenla were ruled by people who later became known as Cambodian. These states grew slowly in size and power in the fertile Mekong delta. They came under the control of the Saliendra dynasty on the island of Java to the south whose political and religious traditions originated in India.

The birth of the Khmer kingdom of Angkor dates from 800 AD when King Jayavarman II returned from Java to unify the people of what is today Cambodia. He established his capital at present-day Angkor. Following the teaching of his Brahmin priest, Jayavarman established himself as the *deva-raja* (god-king) and set the tone for Cambodian political thought that prevailed well into modern times. The temples built to venerate the gods, and also the monarch, were dedicated to either Siva, the Destroyer, or Vishnu, the Preserver. This pattern endured until the 13th century when Buddhist monks from Sri Lanka introduced the Theravada sect of Buddhism, which took hold and is today Cambodia's major religion. The temples were built for the gods and not the people. In the area around Angkor alone, more than 600 temples were built. The palaces of the kings were constructed of wood and no trace remains of them except for their depiction in the stone bas-reliefs of temples that offer insight into the life of the ancient city.

Angkor Wat

The riches of Angkor were built on conquest and wise water management. The history of Cambodia is a story of almost constant warfare, usually between the kingdom of Champa to the east and the Siamese (later Thai) to the west. Eventually the Cham were supplanted by the Vietnamese who over the centuries advanced southward along the coast of the South China Sea from Hanoi. This led to direct conflict with the Khmer, a situation little changed in modern times. As the early kings of Angkor moved westward they entered the domain of the Buddhist Mon in the lower Chao Phraya river valley, now in Thailand. Gradually the Siamese moved south into this area out of southern China, replacing the Mon and facing off against the Khmer.

The rich rice land around Angkor is nurtured by the Mekong River which feeds into the Tonle Sap via the Tonle Sap River. This unique waterway changes its course twice a year as the water level rises in the monsoon season, when the lake triples in volume. As the water level drops, the river reverses its course and drains back into the Mekong, which meets the Tonle Sap at Phnom Penh, Cambodia's present capital.

Aerial view of the fertile ricefields of Battambang province

There are 20,000 stone ruins scattered across the lands that used to be the Khmer empire, now located in Cambodia, Thailand, and Laos. They give testimony to the greatness of the builders of the ancient empire with its well-developed road system linking the outer provinces with the capital. All roads led to Angkor. This was a puzzle to the European explorers who excavated the sites in the 19th and 20th centuries. For a long time they asked, "who built these great monuments? Surely not the rustic Khmer who now lived among them?"

The pearl of the Angkor temples is the 10th century Banteay Srei, arguably the most beautiful of any ancient structure in Cambodia. Located only fifteen miles north of Angkor, it is a miniature temple compared to the massive works at Angkor. It is executed in pink sandstone with intricate carvings and is the only major temple not to have been built by a king. It is the work of a court official, a scholar and philanthropist, who dedicated the temple to Siva. The temple was discovered by French archaeologists in 1914. The striking beauty of the carvings was too much for

From left:
Finely carved lintels
at Banteay Srei.

Pink Sandstone
apasara.

the writer André Malraux who stole four stone carvings of the semi-divine nymphs that are the hallmark of Banteay Srei. Malraux was caught and convicted and the carvings were recovered; Malraux went on to become France's Minister of Culture. Art theft is still a major problem in Cambodia and many of the country's finest works of art are found today in western museums.

Not far from Banteay Srei is Phnom Kulen, the holiest mountain in Cambodia. It was here in 802 that Jayavarman II, the founder of Angkor, declared himself the deva-raja. He commissioned elaborate carvings of Vishnu in the rock floor of the river after having the water temporarily diverted. Jayavarman chose this spot at the top of a series of waterfalls as his bathing site. Court officials were permitted to bathe at a lower level and commoners bathed at the bottom. Today anyone can bathe at the king's spot, which has become a popular weekend picnic site for locals. A nearby attraction is the sixteenth-century Buddhist monastery of Preah Ang Tho, which is famed for a fifty-foot long image of the reclining Buddha, carved into the top of a sixty-foot high boulder. For many years the rugged mountain area around Phnom Kulen was a Khmer Rouge stronghold and has been open to the public only since 1999. It is unwise to wander off paths and roads as land mines are still a danger here, as in many of Cambodia's border areas.

Family bathing at the top of a waterfall at Phnom Kulen with ancient carvings in the stone under the water. It was here that Jayavarman II, the founder of Angkor, declared himself the deva-raja (god-king) in 802 AD.

Monk praying at a large reclining buddha image at Phnom Kulen

Artisans repair an image of the standing Buddha at Angkor

Today Angkor is largely restored but remains a work in progress. It is the foremost tourist attraction in Southeast Asia and has been declared a UNESCO World Heritage site. Bernard-Philippe Groslier, a man who followed in his father's pioneering footsteps and devoted his life to the study and preservation of Angkor Wat, wrote. "It is the best-known Khmer temple and the unique embodiment of the spirit of Angkor, constituting as it does the most perfect expression…of Khmer art. It is not an exaggeration to say that every stone of Angkor Wat…bears the stamp of perfection."

Buddhist monk at Angkor Wat

The great size and attention to detail of the temple is awe-inspiring. Every stone is carved with great skill and care. The galleries contain 1,200 square meters of bas-reliefs depicting epic Hindu tales besides documenting the grandeur and history of the Khmer and their achievements. This masterpiece is the work of Suryamarman II who expanded the size of the empire as the expense of his ally Champa whom he betrayed and conquered. Construction of Angkor Wat began around 1119 and took thirty years to complete. The temple was dedicated to Vishnu but may well have also been built as a mausoleum for the king himself.

Bas relief of soldiers marching at Angkor Wat.

A temple finished by Suryavarman and that is the source of continuing dispute with Thailand is Preah Vihear, perhaps the most inaccessible of all Cambodian temples. It sits atop a 518-meter (1,700-foot) cliff on the Dangkrek escarpment on the Thai-Cambodian border. The problem is that the high ground belongs to Thailand and the temple belongs to Cambodia, thanks to a World Court decision of 1962. It is very difficult to reach the temple from the Cambodian side but easy from Thailand. Tensions between the two countries have made the ruins difficult to visit, a pity because the view from the temple to the plains of northern Cambodia below is spectacular.

Stone carved bas relief at Angkor Wat.

Temple of Preah Vihear on the Thai-Cambodian border. The temple was given to Cambodia in a World Court decision made in 1962.

Bayon temple at Angkor

Giant roots invade the Temple of Ta Phrom, Angkor

Suryavarman's victory over the Cham sowed the seeds of their revenge. In 1177 the Cham launched a surprise attack on Angkor from the water. Out of the chaos rose a king in Cambodia who was able to repel the Cham and restore order. He was Jayavarman VII, already sixty when he ascended the throne. He was a builder and a Buddhist and is regarded as one of the greatest kings of the Khmer. He rebuilt the capital with a 12.8-km moat around it. At the center of his new city, Angkor Thom, was the Bayon. This great temple has suffered badly over the centuries but its magnificent massiveness endures. Another legacy of Jayavarman was Ta Phrom, which today is one of the most evocative ruins at Angkor with the giant roots of strangler fig trees smothering the stone building. French archeologists have purposefully left the trees in place to show the strength and raw beauty of nature at work.

Temple of Banteay Chhmar
in northwestern Cambodia.

The temple of Banteay Chhmar, another of Jayavarman's commissions, is the largest unrestored temple. It is located in a remote northwest corner of Cambodia near the Thai border about forty-eight km north of Poipet. Like Ta Prohm, the temple is remarkable for its unaltered state as jungle has taken over the site. But unlike Ta Prohm, which is in the middle of the much-visited Angkor park, Banteay Chhmar sits alone in the jungle. Its isolation has meant it is rarely visited, adding to its allure.

Jayavarman is remembered for his good works—he built over one hundred hospitals—but by his time the days of the empire were numbered. The Siamese were gathering strength and Cambodia had been weakened by the depredations of the Cham. In 1431 the Siamese captured Angkor. When they sacked Angkor they not only destroyed and looted the temples, they also removed many of the

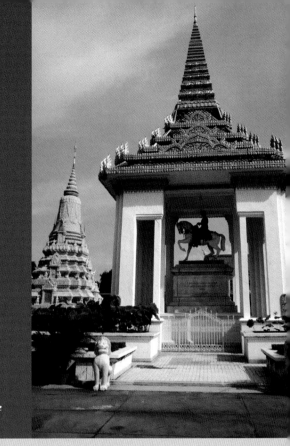

Statue of King Norodom on a horse in the grounds of the Royal Palace, Phnom Penh.

population, including engineers, artisans, and scholars. Many lived out their lives as slaves in Siam. The Khmer empire was effectively ended, and in the following year the Khmer shifted their capital to Phnom Penh at the confluence of the Mekong and Tonle Sap rivers, far from marauding Siamese.

A Cambodian legend says that Phnom Penh was founded in 1372 at a time when the countryside was inundated by monsoon floods. A lady named Penh was living on a small hill on the West bank of the Tonle Sap. One day the floodwaters washed a large koki tree ashore; four bronze images of the Buddha along with an image of Vishnu were found in a hollow of the tree. A wooden sanctuary for the Buddha images was erected on the summit of Penh's hill. This site known as Phnom Don Penh or The Hill of Lady Penh dominates the city and is today a park. The small temple on top is a local shrine. Wild monkeys scamper around the hillside and elephants once again stroll around the base, now carrying tourists and not court officials. Another structure was built lower on the hill for the image of Vishnu.

When Henri Mouhot stumbled on Angkor, Cambodia was under the rule of King Norodom who had been installed by the Siamese and was their unhappy vassal. In 1863 King Norodom sought to end Siam's domination and asked for the

Baquettes of French bread for sale in Phnom Penh.

assistance of the French, who acceded and declared Cambodia to be under the protection of France. Thus, Cambodia joined French Indochina, probably a wise decision as it may have saved the country from being swallowed by the Siamese and disappearing as an independent state. In 1907 the French forced a treaty on the Siamese that returned the rich provinces of Battambang and Siem Reap to Cambodia.

Middle-class house in Phnom Penh surrounded by a fruit and orchid garden.

Under French colonial rule Cambodia enjoyed an era of peace and prosperity as France built an infrastructure of roads, rail, and port facilities. They developed substantial rubber and coffee industries. Phnom Penh took on the look of a provincial French town, with tree-lined boulevards, impressive public works including schools and hospitals, and elegant villas around Wat Phnom in the north part of town. They built a royal palace and national museum for the king along traditional Cambodian architectural lines.

The Throne Hall of the Royal Palace in Phnom Penh

The main structure in the palace is the Throne Hall. Originally constructed in wood in 1869, it was completely rebuilt in 1919 with an elaborate European interior to complement the Asian exterior. To the left of the throne is an impressive statue of King Sisowath, Norodom's successor. Probably the most striking building in the palace is the Dance Sala, an open-air structure constructed on the palace walls looking out onto the river. The most unusual feature of the royal palace is the Iron Building, a gift from Napoleon III of France in the 1870s. Adjacent to the palace grounds is a Buddhist temple used by the recent kings of Cambodia. This is Wat Preah Keo Morokot, which houses a jadeite carving of the Buddha, its most sacred relic. The temple is known as the Silver Pagoda due to the 5,329 tiles of solid silver that cover the floor. The temple is used for royal ceremonies, although monks are not in residence.

Buddha images in the Silver Pagoda; the floor of the pagoda is lined with tiles of pure silver.

Left: Pavilion at the Royal Palace in Phnom Penh where the royal ballet traditionally performed.

Traité
Franco-Siamois
du 15 mars 1907
—
Battambang
Siem-Reap
Sisophon

Statue of a seated King Sisowath at Wat Phnom. The statue was added to complement an existing French memorial.

Courtyard of the National Museum.

Another legacy from the French is the National Museum located next to the Royal Palace. The museum building dates from 1917 and although its style is essentially Khmer, it was designed by George Groslier. Groslier was the principal restorer of Angkor, the first curator of the museum, and the father of Bernard-Philippe Groslier who carried on his father's work until the Khmer Rouge forced him to stop in the early 1970s. The museum opened in 1920 by King Sisowath, was known initially as the Albert Sarrault Museum in honor of a minister of colonies. Many of the best examples of Khmer stone and bronze sculpture were taken to France, but the museum has a collection of more than 14,000 works of art, with no more than one thousand on exhibit at one time. More than one hundred pieces have been added to the collection after being recovered from art thieves, an old and continuing problem in the country. In recent years the museum has been renovated and the collection expanded to include post-Angkor images of the Buddha. The Ethnology

King Sisowath's body was kept in this urn before he was cremated, National Museum, Phnom Penh.

Hall houses relatively recent artifacts including thrones, royal palanquins, and regalia. An interesting relic is the 1920 copper and silver funeral urn of King Sisowath.

The French also brought in large numbers of Vietnamese workers to Cambodia and encouraged Chinese business entrepreneurs to come here. Eventually the Khmer became a minority in their own capital where it was possible to work speaking French, Vietnamese, or Chinese but not Khmer.

The decline of the French in Cambodia began with World War II. French Indochina was occupied by the Japanese for much of the war, followed by a war for independence in neighboring Vietnam. Cambodia was spared in this conflict because Sihanouk sided with the Japanese and refused to fight the French. Faced with defeat in Vietnam, the French granted Cambodia its own independence in

Prince Sihanouk bades farewell to the visiting Chinese premier, 1963.

1953 when it became a constitutional monarchy under Norodom Sihanouk, a great grandson of the Norodom who had invited the French into Cambodia in the 19th century. Sihanouk invited them out.

No sooner had the French left Indochina after their humiliating defeat at Dien Bien Phu in 1954 than a fresh war broke out that pitted North Vietnam against South Vietnam. The United States stepped in and replaced the French in support of the south while China and the Soviet Union bankrolled the north. Sihanouk delayed Cambodia's entry into this conflict for more than a decade by refusing to join either side although he was secretly doing business with the communists. This civil war did not affect Cambodia for more than a decade as Sihanouk delicately walked the tightrope of neutrality. To move soldiers and materiel into the south the North Vietnamese constructed the so-called Ho Chi Minh trail, a network of roads and trails through remote jungle areas of eastern Laos and Cambodia leading into South Vietnam. Sihanouk quietly permitted this violation of neutrality and also permitted the Vietnamese to use Cambodia's deep-sea port at Sihanoukville. At the same time he

A 1974 photo of President Lon Nol (with chain around neck) and army commander General Sosthene Fernandez (to his left).

refused to complain when the United States launched its secret bombing campaign in eastern Cambodia against Vietnamese army sanctuaries. This tilt towards Hanoi upset many in the Cambodian government and on 18 March 1970, while Sihanouk was abroad, he was ousted from power by a unanimous vote in parliament.

Prime Minister Lon Nol ended the monarchy, one of the oldest in the world, and proclaimed the Khmer Republic. Sihanouk went into exile in China and declared his support for the Cambodian communists he had spent years fighting. These were Cambodian communists known as the Khmer Rouge, who were supported by China and North Vietnam. Fighting began as soon as the new republic was proclaimed, and Cambodian found itself involved in the Vietnam War. There were already several North Vietnamese Army (NVA) infantry divisions inside Cambodia protecting the trail. Soon after fighting broke out an NVA regiment captured Angkor but not Siem Reap nearby. The small and poorly equipped Cambodia army was no match for NVA regulars who did the bulk of the fighting in the early years, while the Khmer Rouge grew in numbers and strength.

Khmer Rouge armed patrol on the Thai-Cambodian border, 1979.

American forces made a short incursion into Cambodia at the request of Lon Nol in 1970 but were already in the process of withdrawal from Vietnam and did not stay long. By 1971 all US fighting units had pulled out of Vietnam. In 1973 US bombing in Cambodia ceased as American support of both the Vietnamese and Cambodian governments declined. In April 1975, almost out of ammunition and without American aid, the Khmer Republic ceased to exist when the victorious Khmer Rouge walked into Phnom Penh virtually unopposed.

The Khmer Rouge began by emptying the cities, including the hospitals, prisons, and temples. Former officials and soldiers were shot. To have an education meant a death sentence. The Khmer Rouge quickly confined Sihanouk to his palace in Phnom Penh, his work as a figurehead done. Under their leader Saloth Sar, known as Pol Pot, they sought to remake Khmer society along draconian and radical communist lines. In their five years in power, an estimated two to three million Cambodians lost their lives, in the name of creating a classless society where all one did was

Tourists look at photos of some of the people murdered by the Khmer Rouge at the infamous S-21 prison now called Toul Sleng in Phnom Penh.

An empty room at the Toul Sleng Genocide Museum in Phnom Penh.

work. There were no markets, no schools, no pagodas, no cafes—only communal canteens and sleeping quarters. Families were broken up. Hundreds of thousands managed to flee, mostly to Thailand, where for years the largest concentration of Cambodians in the world was in a refugee camp near Aranyaprathet.

Khmer Rouge soldiers entering Thailand after being pushed out by invading Vietnamese forces, 1979.

A grim reminder of the horrors of the Khmer Rouge is a former school in Phnom Penh that became a prison and interrogation/torture center called S-21 Prison, now known as Tuol Sleng. Meticulous records and photos show that as many as 13,000 people, men, women, and children passed through S-21; only a tiny handful survived. Ironically, many of the victims of S-21 were Khmer Rouge cadres

or sympathizers. The paranoid regime was consuming its own kind. Today S-21 is the Tuol Sleng Genocide Museum. Its visitors are mainly foreign tourists. For Cambodians it is painful place, a place haunted by the spirits of the dead.

The Khmer Rouge also made trouble for their old ally, Vietnam. The Khmer Rouge revolution was a disaster, the economy a mess. The Khmer Rouge blamed their troubles on foreign forces, first the CIA and then the Vietnamese. To draw attention away from their problems, the Khmer Rouge launched border attacks in late 1977 against Vietnam. The Vietnamese, who put the Khmer Rouge in power, were wrong when they thought they could control Pol Pot. The border incidents culminated with a full invasion of Cambodia in December 1978. The Vietnamese quickly pushed the Khmer Rouge out of the cities and into the mountains and jungle on the Thai border where they carried on a guerrilla war. China, the only remaining ally of the Khmer Rouge, responded with their own mini-invasion of northern Vietnam along a 804-km (500-mile) front. This incursion was billed by the Chinese as "punishment" for Vietnam's ouster of the Khmer Rouge. The Chinese did not expect the vigorous defense by the battle-hardened Vietnamese that ensued, and having lost an estimated 20,000 dead within two weeks, the Chinese withdrew.

Thus began a ten-year occupation of Cambodia by Vietnam, the imposition of a puppet regime in Phnom Penh, and a three-sided civil war. This conflict pitted the pro-Vietnamese People's Republic of Cambodia against a loose coalition that included the Chinese-supported Khmer Rouge and an alliance of the United States and some Southeast Asian countries that supported a non-communist coalition of two groups. These included the Khmer People's National Liberation Front under the elderly statesman and former prime minister Son Sann, and a royalist group headed by Sihanouk, who had recanted his support for the murderous Khmer Rouge.

The war ended in 1991 following the withdrawal of Vietnamese forces from Cambodia at the signing of a peace agreement in Paris, which led to United Nations (UN) supervised national elections. Cambodia was again at peace with the Khmer Rouge out of power and the Vietnamese returned to Vietnam. The election was won by Prince Norodom Ranarith, one of Sihanouk's sons. However, supporters of Hun Sen, the prime minister under the Vietnamese and a former Khmer Rouge commander who lost the election threatened a coup d'etat. To prevent a new war the UN buckled and appointed Hun Sen a 'co-prime minister'. When the UN departed Hun Sen made good his earlier threat and led a bloody coup d'etat against his royalist partners and took full power in 1997, a situation that continues today. In 2004 the aging Sihanouk, who had resumed his title as king, abdicated in favor of his son Sihamoni.

Despite the near destruction of Khmer society by the Khmer Rouge, an art form that survived was classical dance. This symbol of Cambodia's royal heritage and ancient civilization and entertainment for the aristocracy was by tradition performed by women. Under Pol Pot, performers of classical dance were hunted down and murdered. An estimated ninety percent of the country's best dancers were killed. With the creation of the Khmer Republic in 1970, the Royal Ballet ceased to exist and since the departure of the Khmer Rouge the focus of dance training has shifted to two government institutions that provide training in dance for young students.

One survivor of the Khmer Rouge purge of dancers is Sophiline Cheam Shapiro who in 1991 co-founded The Khmer Arts Ensemble, an independent dance company that has taken classical dance in Cambodia in a new direction. Not affiliated with the government or any of the government schools, the ensemble is a non-profit organization. Each of its twenty-three full-time salaried dancers is a graduate of the University of Fine Arts, and in addition to performing ancient dances the ensemble dances original dances choreographed by Sophiline such as her 1999 opus Samritechak, an adaptation of Shakespeare's *Othello*. The ensemble trains and performs at the Khmer Arts Theater located at the Centre of Culture and Vipassana in a quiet and verdant setting about eleven-km south of Phnom Penh.

Girls training at the Fine Arts Department's dance school

Dancers practicing at
Khmer Arts Ensemble.

Khmer Arts ensemble dancing.

Revelers dance along the riverside at the Water Festival in Phnom Penh.

Another revival of an ancient tradition, albeit much more raucous, is the Water Festival, which should not be confused with Cambodian New Year which takes place in April and features a lot of water throwing as part of the festivities. This three-day event takes place at the end of the monsoon season, at the time of the full moon, in October or November in Phnom Penh at the confluence of the Mekong, Tonle Sap, and Bassac rivers, and features boat races. The population of the city doubles to over a million as people from the countryside pour into the capital to watch 2,500 rowers from all over the country race 400 boats, some seventy feet long, vie for prizes and glory. Teams from neighboring countries make the festival international. Hundreds of thousands of cheering fans line the banks of the river in front of the Royal Palace as boats race along a one-kilometer course urged on by cheerleaders at the bow of the boats, including some girls dancing. At night the

crowd is entertained by a flotilla of brightly illuminated boats sponsored by various government ministries, followed by fireworks. The festival is timed to coincide with the semi-annual change in the direction of flow of the Tonle Sap as it reverses its course and flows again into the Mekong. The festival pays thanks to the waters that nourish Cambodia and that provide abundant fish.

Phnom Penh is again a bustling and vibrant city trying to shake off its nightmarish recent past. Food is important to the Khmer and they have a rich and spicy cuisine inspired both by India and China. The city's wide boulevards again offer chic French bistros, sidewalk cafes, and other Western restaurants that complement a wide variety of Chinese, Vietnamese, and other Asian fare.

Brightly-lit boats representing the various Cambodian ministries on parade at the water festival.

The crowd line the banks of the
Tonle Sap River in Phnom Penh
for the annual boat races.

Note the offerings in the bow of
the boat at annual water festival,
Phnom Penh.

For shopping in Phnom Penh both tourists and residents flock to the meandering and crowded Toul Tum Poung Market, known to most people as the Russian Market from the days in the 1980s when most Western residents or tourists were Soviet supporters of the Vietnamese-installed government. There are good buys to be found by discerning buyers skilled in the art of good-natured bargaining. One can find genuine antiques and artifacts but these are hidden among many more reproductions or downright fakes. Let the buyer beware. Textiles are a "best buy," from old silk sarongs in rich reds and oranges to modern fabrics and designs from nearby textile factories. The Russian Market is also the place to go for copied software, videos, and compact disks.

A good buy
for visitors is
Cambodian silk.

buddhas and buddha heads for
sale at a good price.

An easy day trip from Phnom Penh is a visit to Oudong, a sleepy little town that in the 17th century was the capital of Cambodia but was forsaken by King Norodom in 1866 when he shifted his court to Phnom Penh. The road follows the Tonle Sap River and then turns to the high ground dominated by Phnom Oudong and the renovated Wat Oudong above. There is a festive air at Oudong on weekends when city folk flock to the historical place to buy food specialties from the countryside. These include live turtles, which are prepared in a salad with banana leaves and mint. Another favorite is pickled ants, which are usually eaten as a snack with chilies. Small salty crabs are popular and are served with grilled fish in a green papaya salad. In the rainy season the lowlands around Oudong are in flood and the view from Wat Oudong is spectacular.

Turtles for sale.

Small fresh water crabs for sale; these will probably end up in a salad with spicy green papaya.

Another suggested day trip from Phnom Penh is a visit to Tonle Bati, a small lake thirty-two-km south of the capital. It is popular as a weekend fishing hole for urbanites. It is also the site of a 12th century temple called Ta Phrom built by Jayavarman VII. There is another temple nearby, Phnom Chisor; this is located on the top of a mountain and involves a climb of over 400 steps.

Spicy ants that are consumed as a snack with chillies.

View of the countryside from Wat Oudong. In the background is the flooded Tonle Sap River.

Further afield, the center of beach resorts on the Cambodian coast is Sihanoukville, formerly known as Kompong Som. About 225 km west of Phnom Penh, a pleasant three-hour drive on a good highway, Sihanoukville is the country's major deep-sea port. Many travelers, especially Cambodians, stop at the Pich Nil Pass through low mountains to pay homage to the patron spirit of coastal Cambodia, Ya-Mao. Dozens of spirit houses line the pass where offerings such as bananas, incense, and money can be made. There are numerous legends about the woman, Ya-Mao. One of them says she was the wife of a village chief on the coast near Sihanoukville and that the two were often separated from her home in Koh Kong. During a monsoon season she took a boat to join her husband when a storm came up and she was drowned. But her strong spirit endures and she is revered in the area for her protection of fisherman and, by extension, travelers heading for the coast.

Offerings to Ya-Mao at the
Pich Nil Pass on Highway 4.

In recent years Sihanoukville has become popular among foreign tourists and Cambodians alike for the broad sandy beaches that dot the coast around the port and offshore islands. The most crowded of these is Serendipity Beach, a long tree-lined strip with inexpensive lodging nearby, ocean-front bars and restaurants, and vendors selling snacks, drinks, or offering massages to the travelers who gather on this friendly and affordable beach. More upscale is the privately owned Sokha Beach, which is part of the five-star Sokha Beach Hotel that sets the standard for excellence in and around Sihanoukville, where the beach scene is reminiscent of Thailand thirty years ago.

More laid back than Sihanoukville is the quaint and quiet town of Kampot to the east, also on the Gulf of Thailand. Its evocative French colonial architecture mixed with Chinese shop-houses and quiet streets offer a solitude not found at the more robust tourist scene at Sihanoukville. Just beyond Kampot is Kep, known as Kep-sur-mer in the days of the French, when this idyllic little town was Cambodia's premier seaside getaway for the country's elite. Sihanouk and many member of the royal family had weekend villas here for weekend soirées. Much of the town was destroyed by the Khmer Rouge and many of the grand villas are today abandoned shells. The town, however, still retains it beauty with lush tree-lined streets along the water.

This serene and remote setting is perfect for the boutique resort Knai Bang Chatt that advertises itself as "the ultimate private experience". It is so private that there is no sign identifying it. Its owners say this is not a hotel but rather a private residence for rent on an exclusive basis. Comprised of three vintage art deco-style villas on the water, this elegant and subdued resting-place is a favorite for the rich and famous who want to escape the crowds, a gem that is putting Kep back on the map.

The classic way to tour Cambodia, dating from the days of Angkor, was by boat. Before roads were built and later paved, the country had a network of coastal and inland waterways. In the 1930s there was a twice-weekly steamer service plying between Bangkok and Cambodian coastal ports including Kep. Two steamers sailed twice weekly throughout the year except for the monsoon season. There was also a service of river steamers running year round from Saigon (now Ho Chi Minh City) up to Phnom Penh and on to Viam near Siem Reap. This service operated three times a week; first-class passage to Phnom Penh cost US$27.50.

Serendipity beach parasailing.

Seaside pavilions for visitors at Kampot.

Wide view of Knai bang Chatt Resort.

Riverboats still ply Cambodian waters with varying levels of comfort, cost, and safety. Perhaps the most comfortable and evocative of them, and a throwback to the days of colonial river travel is the Pandaw Cruises, with three boats on the Mekong, operated by the Irrawaddy Flotilla Company. This firm is a direct descendent of the 19th century company that once had 600 riverboats in Burma. It now has an international fleet and this boat has been cruising in Cambodian waters since 2003. Newly built in the style of the old riverboats and outfitted in Burma teak, the Pandaw plies between Saigon and Angkor Wat with numerous stops along the way for sightseeing. Life on the rivers is rich and fascinating and a much better way to see the country than by plane, car, or bus.

As the tourism industry develops in Cambodia and the infrastructure supporting it expands. more and more places will open to visitors. The Mekong River town of Kratie is a good example. It is a six-hour boat ride up the river from Phnom Penh to this pleasant town. Or consider a longer ride by car over good roads through Kompong Cham, across the Mekong on a new bridge, and past vast rubber plantations. Kratie is already a favorite stop with budget travelers who don't mind a little extra effort to find new places with good prices. There are a couple of attractions, one of them the Irrawaddy dolphins that live in the waters around Kratie, a rarity on the Mekong. Another is Sambor Falls about twenty-four-km to the north. This is actually a cataract that prevents passage on the river in low water but is very scenic at any time of year.

Fishing boats tied up along the banks of the Tonle Sap River.

Sidewalk café in Kratie.

Tourism is developing in the mountains of northeastern Cambodia beyond Kratie where most of the country's ethnic hill-tribe minorities live. It is also home to rare animal species including the kouprey, a large bovine, that has not been seen for many years but is still believed to exist in these remote hills. Another remote area that may develop into a tourist destination is Pailin on the Thai border to the far west. This hilly jungle-clad area is the home of Cambodia's ruby and sapphire mines. It was long a sanctuary of the Khmer Rouge and several of their former leaders still live there. The region is notorious for its malaria and also land mines, a legacy of the late civil war, and travel there is only for the hardy.

Shopper buying
jackfruit at the
kratie central
market.

Kratie central market.

Despite the horrors of the Khmer Rouge, Cambodia is once again rebounding from tragedy and is rebuilding. Its magnificent ancient temples make it a must stop for any visitor interested in the rich history of the region. Sidewalk cafes and fine dining have returned to Phnom Penh. Seaside resorts are springing up with accommodations for every budget. The Cambodian people are warm and welcoming. Theravada Buddhism is flourishing. Traditional arts and crafts are being revived. Cambodia has a new king. He is an intellectual and a talented dancer who spent much of his life in France. He reigns over a nation with an elderly civilization and a youthful population that looks to the future with hope and optimism.

Fisherman and wife inspect their haul
near Sambor on the Mekong River.

CAMBODIA

History

A sergeant on the Parachute Brigade of the Cambodian army during a battle at Kilometer 6 north of Phnom Penh a few weeks before the end of the war in 1975. The battalion, normally 500 strong, was down to 52 men.

KPNLF troops training at a
jungle site in Thailand, 1990.

KPNLF troops at Banteay
Chhmar temple in north
western Cambodia, 1991.

American diplomat Timothy Carney explains to Khmer Rouge soldiers that they are inside Thailand.

A 1991 photo of KPNLF and pro-Sihanouk leaaders at a KPNLF ceremony in northwestern Cambodia. These two non-communist groups fought against the Vietnamese puppet government in Cambodia until a Paris peace agreement ended the civil war in 1991.

Khmer Rouge patrol inside
Thailand, 1979. Man at right
carries a hoe which is the method
of execution by the KR.

Phnom Penh cyclo drivers
waiting for fares, 1963.

Khmer Peoples National Liberation Front
troops being entertained by dancers from
a refugee camp in Thailand, 1991. Photo
taken at KPNLF HQ inside Cambodia.

CAMBODIA
Arts and Culture

'Standing guard', carved
sandstone relief at Banteay Srei.

Lintel in danger of collapse at the temple of Banteay Chhmar in the jungle of northwestern Cambodia.

Last light on a finely carved building at Ta Phrom Temple, Angkor.

Detail in pink sandstone at Banteay Srei.

Stone carving at the 10th century temple of Banteay Srei north of Angkor.

Stone demons, some with replacement heads, at the causeway to Angkor Thom, Angkor.

Bullet holes from Vietnamese occupiers in a stone statue at Angkor.

Stone carvings of apasaras at Angkor Wat.

Khmer Arts Ensemble dancer
at Ta Khmau with backdrop of
Bayon-style stone heads.

Stone carving at the Tonle Bati temple constructed by Jayavarman VII in the 12th century, 20 miles from Phnom Penh.

Stone statue in front of the
National Museum, Phnom Penh.

Statue of Hindu deity Yama in the courtyard of the National Museum.

Bronze elephant in front of the National Museum in Phnom Penh.

The Silver Pagoda in the Royal
Palace grounds, Phnom Penh.

The Iron Pavilion, a gift of
Napoleon III of France to King
Norodom in 1870. It is situated in
the Royal Palace in Phnom Penh.

Buddhist temple at Sambor on the banks of the Mekong River.

Mural in the grounds of the Silver Pagoda, Phnom Penh.

Painting of girls bathing at a wat (temple) at Sambor.

CAMBODIA

People

Two boys beaming happily in the ruins of a temple at Angkor.

Woman with head covered by
a krama and her little boy
near Sihanoukville.

Muslim man of the ethnic Cham
community near Phnom Penh.

Female caddies wait for clients at the golf course near Phnom Penh.

Cambodian tourists visit Angkor Wat.

This elderly gentleman is the
self-appointed, unpaid, sweeper
of Ta Phrom temple, Angkor.

Woman takes a break from tending to a rice field located east of Phnom Penh.

Village girl with protecting krama cloth on her head near the temple of Banteay Chhmar in northwestern Cambodia.

In Phnom Penh the passenger sits
in front and driver sits behind.

Thumbs-up for number one service.

Cambodian family during
a visit to Angkor Wat.

CAMBODIA
Daily Life

Two monks stand in front
of an Angkor temple.

Monk at Angkor Wat.

Taking a rest in a
doorway at Angkor Wat.

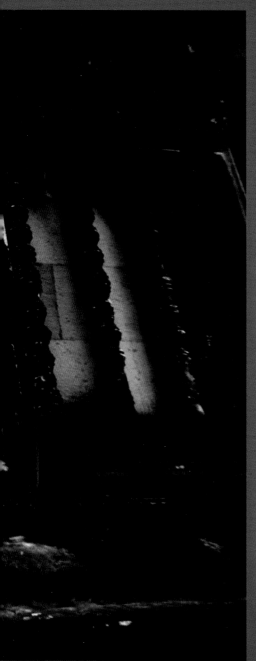

Young novice buddhist monks with freshly shaven heads walk along a road near Mimot rubber plantation close to Vietnam.

Young boy hunting frogs with a crossbow at Angkor with the ruins of Pre Rup temple behind him.

The motorbike is the main form of transportation in Phnom Penh, ferrying everyone from buddhist monks to entire families.

Farmer drives his ox cart down
a dusty road near Thma Pouk,
northwestern Cambodia.

Transporting new mattresses
by motorbike near Takeo.

Furniture being delivered to
market by motorbike near
Kompong Cham.

Life in rural Cambodia moves at
the pace of the ox cart.

Public transport in Phnom Penh.
A motorcycle pulls a passenger-
carrying trailer known as a
remorque to the French.

Passengers crowd a small truck as they head for the Water Festival in Phnom Penh.

Eggseller waiting for
customers in Sisophon,
Western Cambodia.

Women cutting rice by hand near
Snoul on the Vietnamese border.

Traffic congestion near Kampot as
water buffaloes are taken to market.

Elephants for hire at Angkor.

Tourists watch children playing
in the moat at Angkor Wat.

Fisherman casts his net into the Mekong near Kratie.

Children on boat near Siem Reap.

Floating village on the
Tonle Sap near Siem Reap.

This humble home on the Tonle Sap River floods during the rainy season but it has several television antennas to provide entertainment on normal days.

Woman selling wild honey and small crabs at Oudong market.

Hot off the grill, these river
fishes could accompany the small
crab in the papaya salad.

Hot sticky rice makes a tasty meal.

Free range chickens for sale at the Russian Market.

Fresh fish from the Mekong
at this riverside market.

Cambodians praying at the image of a reclining Buddha in the ruins of an Angkor temple.

Open pit mining for blue sapphires at Pailin on the border of Thailand.

CAMBODIA

Nature

Sundown on the river at Siem Reap. The town is 6km from Angkor and means "Crush the Siamese".

Cambodian pond with lotus flower.

Flowers in the garden of
Phnom Penh residence.

About the Author

Barry Broman first worked in Cambodia in 1963 as a photographer for the Associated Press. Ten years later he served in the American embassy in Phnom Penh. Educated at the University of Washington, he has written and photographed numerous books on Asian subjects. He is also a documentary film producer and resides with his wife Betty Jane in Kirkland, Washington.

Photo by Matt Franjola